Incredible Indians

An Iconic Journey from A to Z

Anish & Kanchi Doshi

Illustrated by Steffi Stanley

DEDICATED TO MADHUKANT & CHANDRIKA KACHARIA WHO INSPIRE THEIR GREAT-GRANDCHILDREN TO...

"LIVE HONORABLY, GENEROUSLY, AND WITH INTEGRITY."

SPECIAL THANKS

We are eternally grateful to our families, especially our parents. They taught us about love, history, culture, respect, and so much more. To us, they are the most incredible Indians!

INCREDIBLE INDIANS
Copyright © 2021 by Anish & Kanchi Doshi
Illustrations Copyright © 2021 by Anish & Kanchi Doshi

All rights reserved. This book or any portion thereof may not be reproduced or used in any manner whatsoever without the express written permission of the publisher except for the use of brief quotations in a book review. Although the authors have made every effort to ensure that the information in this book was correct, the authors do not assume and hereby disclaim any liability to any party for any loss, damage, or disruption caused by errors or omissions, whether such errors or omissions result from negligence, accident, or any other cause.

ISBN: 978-0-578-32872-0

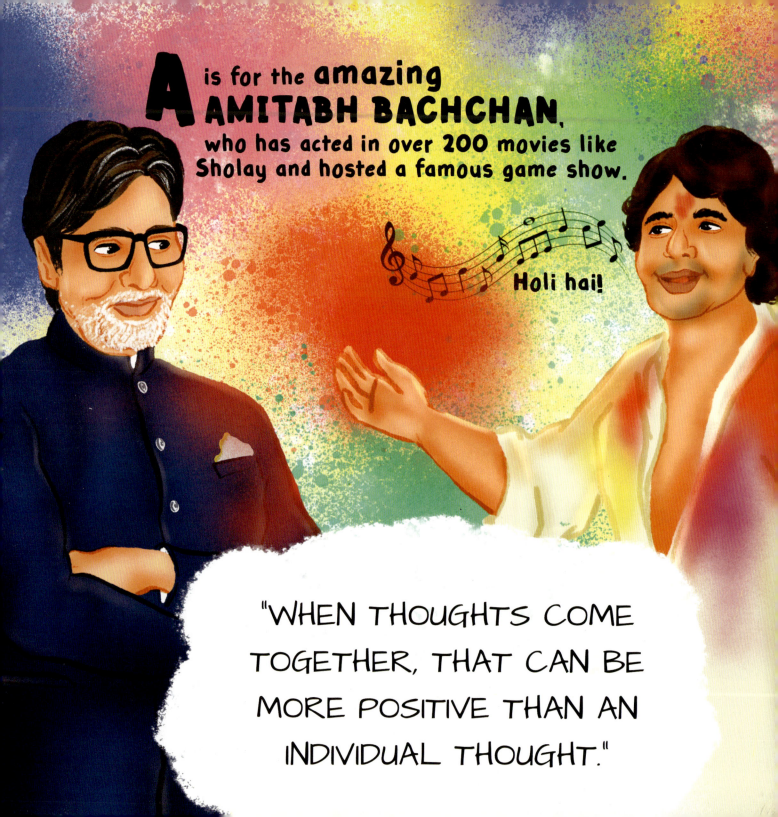

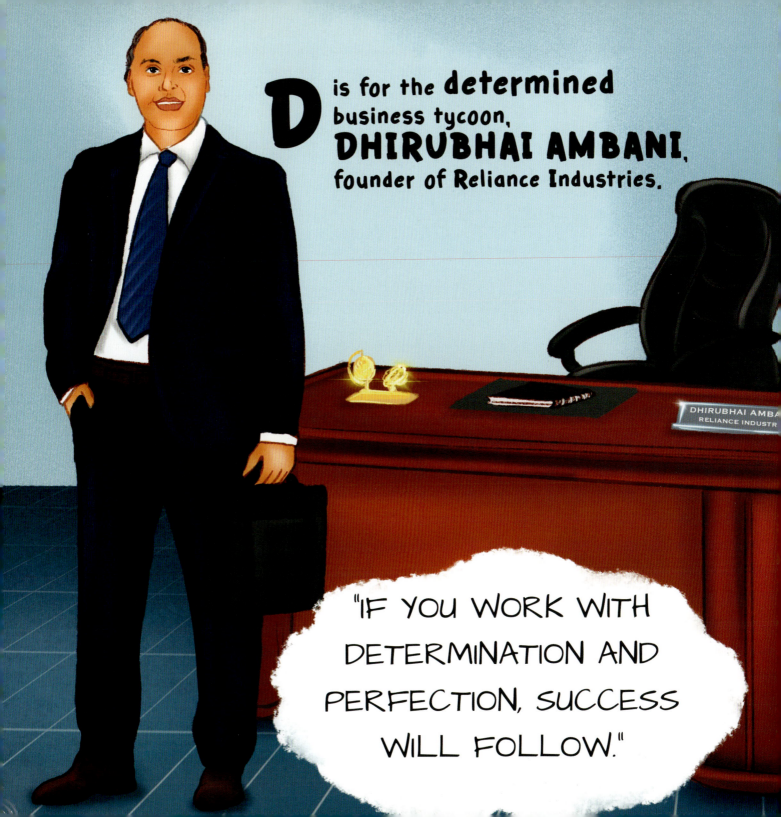

NEWS
FAREED ZAKARIA

F is for the **fearless** author and journalist, **FAREED ZAKARIA**, who inspires change globally.

"I GREW UP IN THE WORLD WHERE EVERYTHING SEEMED POSSIBLE."

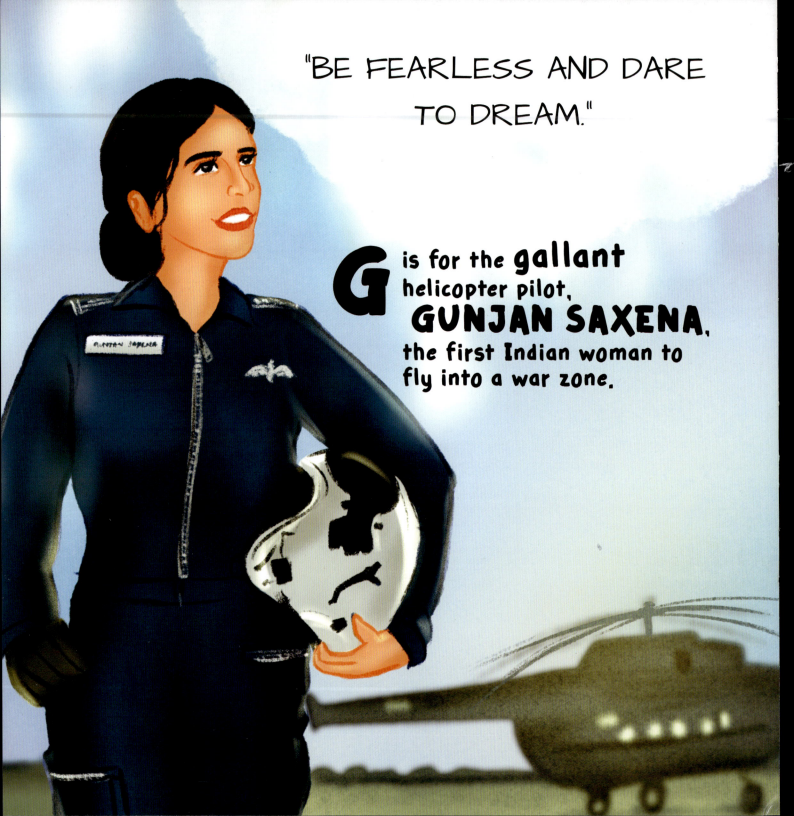

J is for the judicious **JAWAHARLAL NEHRU**, India's first prime minister, whose birthday is celebrated as Children's Day as a tribute to his love for them.

"CITIZENSHIP CONSISTS IN THE SERVICE OF THE COUNTRY."

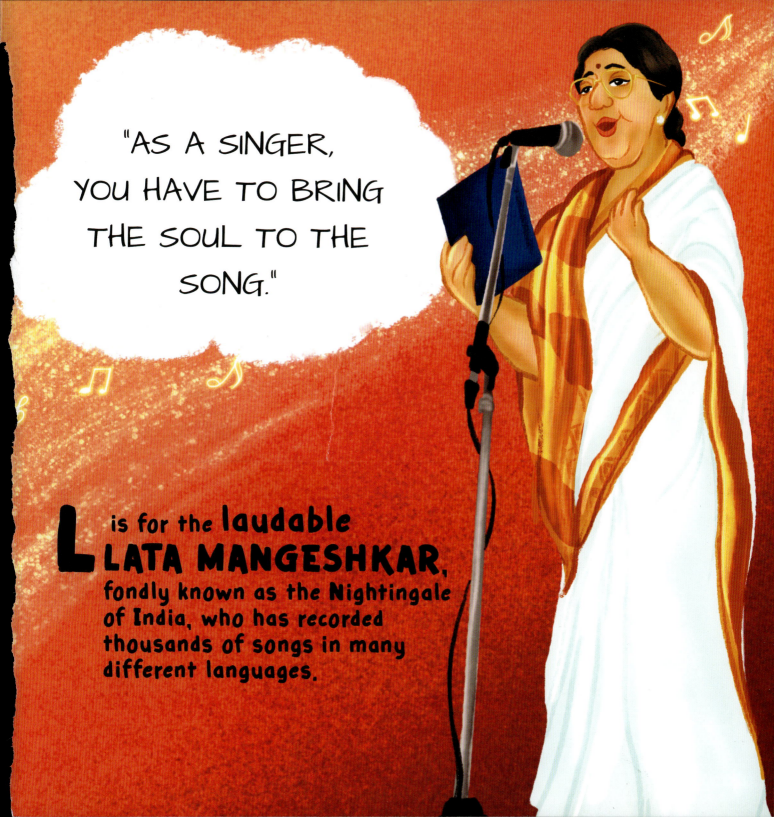

N is for the **notable** javelin thrower, **NEERAJ CHOPRA**, who is the first Indian athlete to win an Olympic gold medal in track and field.

"GIVE YOUR BEST. NEVER FEAR THE OPPOSITION."

P is for the **popular** and **poised PRIYANKA CHOPRA**, former Miss World, actress, feminist and philanthropist.

"THERE IS ONLY ONE YOU SO UNDERSTAND WHO YOU ARE AND YOUR UNIQUENESS."

Q is for the **quick-witted QUEEN OF JHANSI** (Rani Laxmibai), who bravely trained her own army and fought for independence in **1857**.

"I SHALL NOT SURRENDER MY JHANSI!"

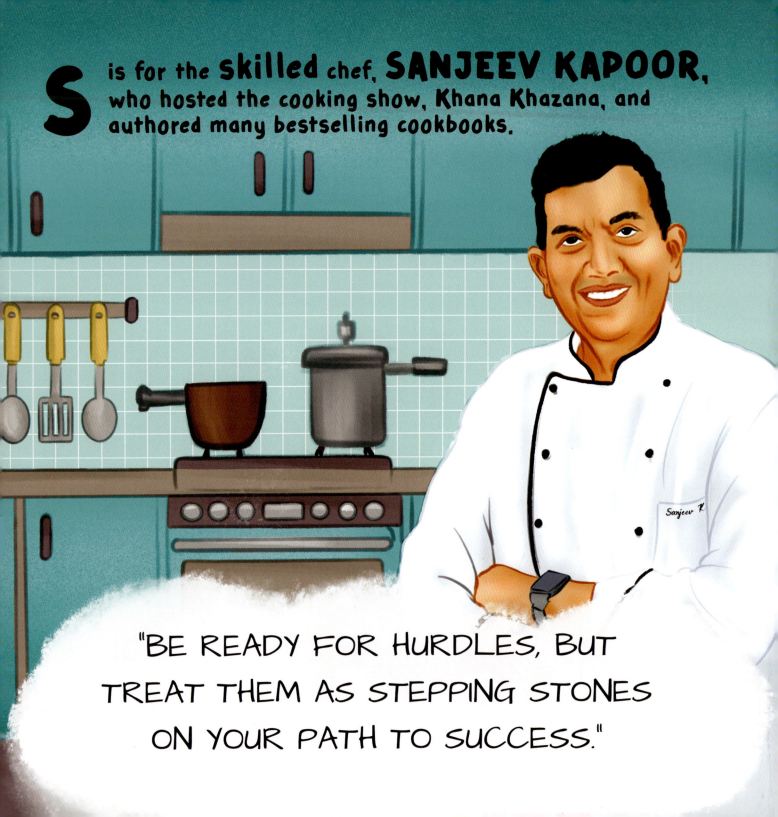

T is for the tender-hearted Teresa of Calcutta, "MOTHER TERESA", who dedicated her life to caring for the poor and the sick.

"SPREAD LOVE EVERYWHERE YOU GO. LET NO ONE EVER COME TO YOU WITHOUT LEAVING HAPPIER."

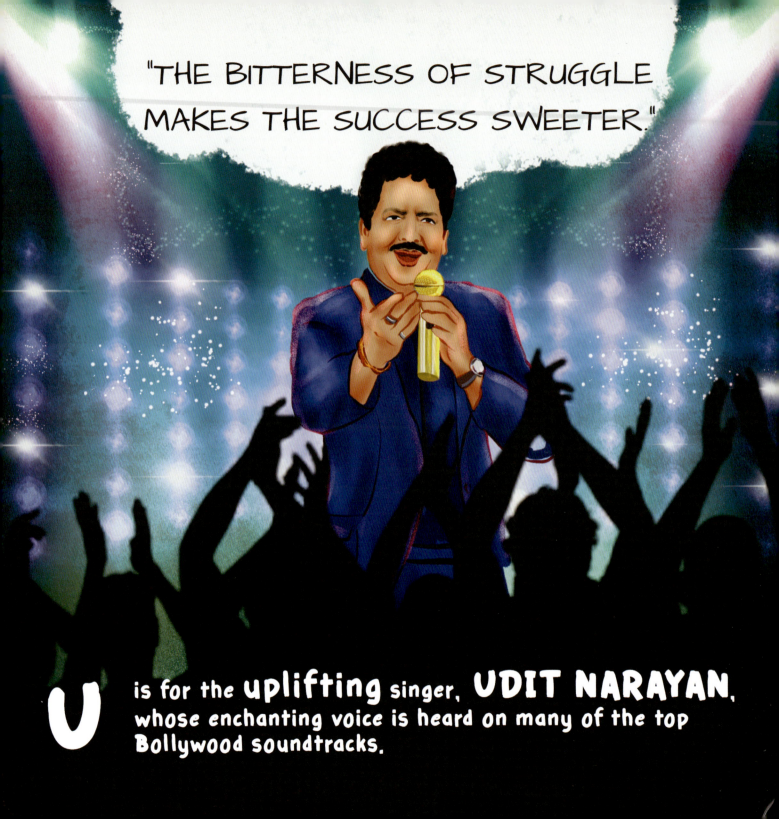

"THE BITTERNESS OF STRUGGLE MAKES THE SUCCESS SWEETER."

U is for the uplifting singer, UDIT NARAYAN, whose enchanting voice is heard on many of the top Bollywood soundtracks.

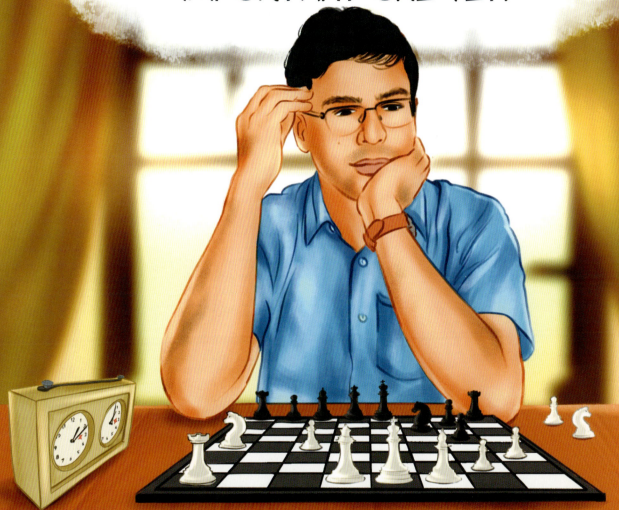

"EACH MATCH I PLAY IS THE MOST IMPORTANT ONE YET."

V is for the **victorious** chess grandmaster, **VISWANATHAN ANAND**, who is a five-time world chess champion.

W is for the **wonderful WENDELL RODRICKS**, fashion designer, environmentalist and social activist.

"TAKE DESIGNS OUT OF YOUR OWN CULTURE, HEART AND SOUL AND PRESENT SOMETHING NEW THAT MAKES YOU STAND OUT FROM THE REST OF THE WORLD."

"I HAVE FAILED MORE TIMES THAN HAVE SUCCEEDED, BUT NEVER GAVE UP AND NEVER WILL GIVE UP UNTIL MY LAST BREATH."

Y is for the **youthful** cricket player and resilient cancer survivor, **YUVRAJ SINGH,** who miraculously hit six sixes in a single over of cricket.

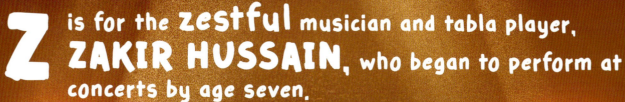

Z is for the **zestful** musician and tabla player, **ZAKIR HUSSAIN**, who began to perform at concerts by age seven.

"EVERY TIME YOU STEP ON TO THE STAGE, YOU LEARN SOMETHING WHICH HELPS YOU GROW. YOU'RE ALWAYS A STUDENT."